T0359622

The Right Tools for the Job

Written by Sarah O'Neil

Flying Start
to Literacy®

Contents

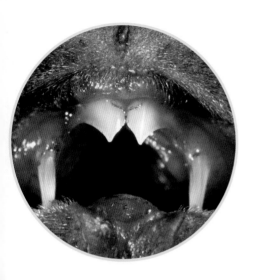

Introduction

All animals need food to survive. Getting food is not always easy but all animals have the body parts they need to get their food and to eat it.

They use these body parts as tools.

Chapter 1
Animals that eat plants

Many animals eat plants. Some eat leaves, others eat fruit and seeds. Some animals eat the wood and bark from plants.

But some plants can be hard to eat and hard to reach. The animals that eat them have the right body parts to help them.

Beavers

Beavers eat the bark from trees. They also eat grass and leaves.

They have long, sharp front teeth that help them to gnaw through the hard bark on small trees. As they gnaw through the bark their teeth get worn down.

A beaver's teeth never stop growing.

A beaver can cut down more than 250 trees in a year.

Giraffes

Giraffes eat leaves that grow on tall trees. These leaves are high above the ground.

Giraffes have long necks that help them to reach these leaves.

Giraffes often eat leaves from trees that have long sharp thorns. These thorns stop many animals from eating the leaves.

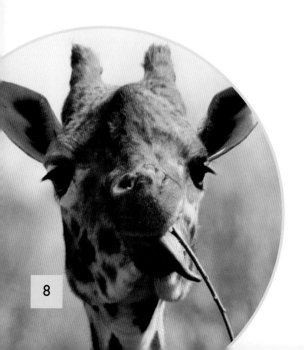

Giraffes can move their tongues around the thorns on these trees and eat the soft leaves without getting pricked by the thorns.

9

Hummingbirds

Hummingbirds eat nectar
from flowers. The nectar
is in the centre of the flower.

A hummingbird has a long, thin
beak and a long, grooved tongue that
it puts into the flower. The nectar
sticks to its grooved tongue.

Hummingbirds are the only birds that can hover.

Hummingbirds can beat their wings more than 200 times in one second. When they beat their wings this fast, they can stay in the one place in the air without falling. This is called hovering.

Hummingbirds need to hover above some flowers to get the nectar.

Chapter 2
Animals that eat meat

Many animals eat other animals.
The animals they eat are called prey.

But some animals are hard to catch and eat. Animals that eat them have the body parts they need to catch and eat their food.

12

Vampire bats

Vampire bats drink the blood of animals such as cows, pigs, horses and birds.

Vampire bats have sensors in their noses. The sensors help the bats to find where the blood is closest to an animal's skin. Vampire bats bite a small hole in the animal's skin and then drink its blood.

Spiders

Spiders eat insects and other small animals. When a spider catches its prey, it uses its fangs to put poison into the animal. The poison either kills the animal or stops it from moving while the spider eats it.

Spiders do not have teeth so they
cannot bite or chew their food.

Spiders eat by sucking out the liquids
in the bodies of the animals they catch.
They do not eat the hard, outer shells.

Anteaters

Anteaters cannot see very well but they have a very good sense of smell. This helps them to find the ants and termites that they eat.

Anteaters use their strong front legs and long, sharp claws to break open ant or termite nests.

Anteaters
eat up to
20,000 ants
every day.

When the nest is open, anteaters poke their long, thin snouts into the nest and lick up the ants or termites with their long, sticky tongues. Anteaters do not have teeth so they swallow the ants whole.

17

Chapter 3
Animal scavengers

Some animals are scavengers. Scavengers are animals that eat food that is dead and rotting. They have the right body parts to find their food and to eat it.

Turkey vultures

Turkey vultures are scavengers. They eat animals that have died, but they have to find them first.

Turkey vultures have large wings. They use their wings to glide high above the ground looking for food. They also have good eyesight and a good sense of smell. This helps them to find their food from the air.

Turkey vultures are one of the few birds that have a sense of smell.

19

Hyenas

Hyenas are scavengers too. They often eat the bodies of animals that have died.

Hyenas have very strong jaws and teeth. They use their teeth to break an animal's body into smaller pieces.

Hyenas have a strong acid in their stomachs. This means that they can eat every part of another animal including the skin, teeth, horns and bones.

Chapter 4
The right tools for the job

Animals have the body parts they need to get food. These are the right tools for the job.

Animal	Food	Tools
Beaver	bark, leaves and grass	• teeth
Giraffe	leaves	• long neck • long tongue
Hummingbird	nectar from flowers	• long, thin beak • grooved tongue • fast-beating wings

Animal	Food	Tools
Spider	insects	• fangs with poison in them
Vampire bat	blood	• sensors • sharp teeth
Anteater	ants, termites	• sharp claws • long snout • sticky tongue
Turkey vulture	dead animals	• strong wings • good sense of smell • good eyesight
Hyena	dead animals	• strong jaws and teeth • acid in its stomach

Conclusion

Animals have many
ways of getting their
food. Each animal
has body parts that
help it to find, catch
and eat its food.